Khadijah goes to School

helping yourself and helping other people™

2nd Edition

Education means you help yourself.
Now you can help other people.

A story about **You**...

no matter what
no matter where
I tell you I do not scare
Knowledge is my witness
I seek you in the thickness
for I am not too old
for I am not too young
I am only a student
my journey just begun...

by studentasim ↳™

pictures by Zayd Hussain, Yusra Hussain, Sayf Hussain, and Aneesa Hussain.

The Opening...

khadijahgoestoschool.com

blished in Canada by LogixPlayer Inc. Printed in Canada.
ail: publisher@logixplayer.com

ng *Khadijah goes to School* to your classroom, library, organization and family.
y online: khadijahgoestoschool.com/shop

™ is a symbol and logo created by and representative of
➔ Asim Hussain (studentasim). It is a registered trademark.

rary and Archives Canada Cataloguing in Publication

ssain, Asim, author
    Khadijah goes to school / by Asim Hussain ; illustrated by Zayd
ssain, Yusra Hussain, Sayf Hussain, Aneesa Hussain. -- 2nd edition.

story about you, 2369-0100)

ued in print and electronic formats.
N 978-0-9869099-3-1 (pbk.).--ISBN 978-0-9869099-4-8 (epub).--
N 978-0-9869099-5-5 (mobi)

    1. Education--Social aspects. 2. Life skills. 3. Conduct of life. I. Hussain,
yd, illustrator II. Hussain, Yusra, illustrator III. Hussain, Sayf, illustrator
Hussain, Aneesa, illustrator V. Title. VI. Series: Hussain, Asim. Story about you

191.H88 2015   370.11'5   C2015-901787-4
                                                    C2015-901788-2

This is for the People of Now
This is for the People of Tomorrow
It's just some Words
Another student can Follow
When You pass the Learn
And give Them a Turn
You establish a Chain
It's Good You Gain
Timeless Your Deeds
The minds You Feed...

uthor's Note: By the Will of Allah (God), the 2nd edition is here! The 1st edition was released in 2011. Fast forward 4 years later, it's been an credible journey of discovery and interaction meeting so many of you and sharing ideas dear to me. It's taken a whole year to produce this dition after much reflection. I wish to share *Khadijah goes to School* with the world and I hope there is something you take away from this ody of work. First, a warm thank you and salute to those who believed in me through this journey, there were lots of times when things weren't asy. A special thank you to my family for being extra patient and supportive. Many thanks to the media for giving me a chance to share my ork. Lastly, I would like to personally thank a few key early adopters; Professor Larry Swartz (OISE, U of T), Professor David Booth (OISE, U of T), : Nadeem Memon (Razi Education), Qaiser Ahmad (TDSB), Dilawar Alvi (TDSB), Amer Meknas, Taha Ghayyur (Sound Vision), Susan Cole (Now Magazine), Habeeb Alli, rlo Cabrera (TDSB), Victoria Moreno (Toronto Women's Bookstore), Fawad Shaikh (TDSB), Jamaal Rogers, Malaika Ghayyur, Elvira Hopper, Junaid Shah, Zeshan Syed, ndra Clarke (Peel), Michelle Perrone-Bonavita (Peel), and Kevin White (Peel) for believing in me and giving me a chance to share my work and gain valuable feedback. before, this is a humble contribution to Canada and wherever else this book may go. To many more years of KGTS Inshallah God Willing! It's been an honour.

My name is Khadijah.

It's my first year at

Olive Tree Public School.

I transferred here from my old school.

I've never heard of this school before, but my parents tell me I'll do just fine.

Everyone tells me it's important to go to school. Sometimes I wonder

why.

Every time I ask, I get the same answer:

"Don't be silly, you go to school because you learn so so so much."

My Parents tell me I'll have fun. It's just a matter of time.

It's the **1st** week of school.
I have these big butterflies
in my tummy every single day.

I start f e e l i n g
like this when my dad is driving me,
even before arriving at school.

"MISS, I have butterflies in my tummy." I tell the teacher.

"How come, Khadijah?" asks the teacher.

"Because I don't like school; I don't feel like I belong here."

"Many students feel the same way you do, at a new school. I will help you, okay

"But aren't you going to say, don't be silly, you go to school because you learn so so so much

"Whoever said that just means learning is for everyone," replies the teache

It's the **2nd** week of school.

"Baba!

Some kids told me there are

pink

monkeys

hiding in the classroom."

"Do you believe everything you hear?"

"Baba, but that's what I heard."

"Well you have some thinking to do then. Now come on, otherwise you're going to be late."

"Miss, are pink monkeys real?"

"No..." the teacher pauses. "But think of pink monkeys like the **unknown**."

"The **unknown**?"

"Yes. The **unknown can be**

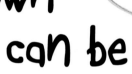

fun and curious."

don't be silly

you go to school because

you learn so so so much

"Well, I **don't like** the unknown and I **don't like** school!"

"Khadijah..." starts the teacher.

"I know what you're going to say, don't be silly, you go to school because you learn so so so much."

"Honey, I know you've heard that. Remember, learning is for everyone."

It's the **3rd** week of school and I'm hoping it'll end soon

I remember the summer holidays we just had and all the fun places I visited with my parents.

It's going to be such a looooooooong time until the next summer holidays! **yikes!**

I wish I
didn't have to
go
o school!

"Khadijah, why are you crying?"

"Because I don't like school, I have butterflies in my tummy and the pink monkeys are going to get me. This year will never end!"

don't be silly
you go to school because
you learn so so so much

"Khadijah, you'll be fine. You're new here.

It takes some getting used to. But look at you. You are so brave for coming to a new school! So don't be silly, you go to school because you learn so so so much." The teacher smiles.

Just then, David comes over and asks the teacher a question. He's interested. He listens. This reminds me of something my parents taught me, "...there is no question that's a bad question when you're learning, ask until you **understand**..."

So I start with myself.

All you can do is your best...

Why °°° do I have **butterflies**? My teacher is **kind** and **helpful**.

°°° am I afraid of pink monkeys? Cu ious monkeys could be fun.

°°° am I crying? Summer holidays will come again. I can be patient.

And my teacher said I am brave. I think about this for a moment...

"Miss, why do we **need to** learn **so so so much?**" I ask with a sniffle.

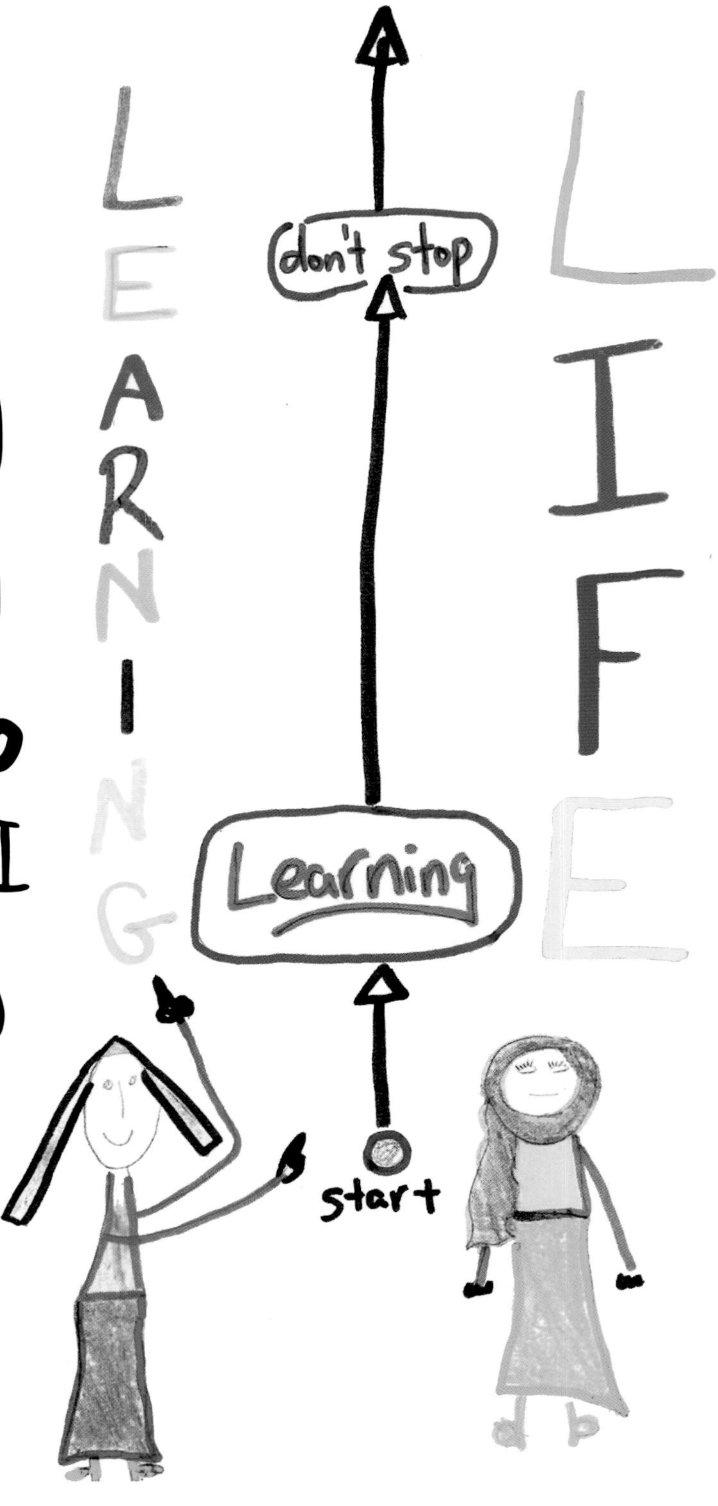

L
E
A
R
N
I
N
G

don't stop

Learning

start

L
I
F
E

"Because learning **is a part of** life," says the teacher.

"What is life?"

"Life is helping yourself and helping other people," replies the teacher.

"And **how** do we start doing that?" I wonder.

"If I told you a **secret,** would you believe it?"

I am surprised. Everything around me stops. My heart starts to race.

"please **tell me.**"

I whisper.

"The Secret of Life..."

My eyes widen as I wait for the teacher to finish.

resima   forà   String read=new String("Read");

funda   הרקא   leggere   itaníík   lasīt

skaityti   чета   чита   les   czytaj   leghje

akíinziikw   llegir   basáha   læse   読む

ukubelenga   ᏓᎦᎳ   پڑھ   Alîha   akhri

ၣးလၣ်   R   dubbisuu   வாசி   0111001001100101011000010110 0100

au   ku-tanga   ukwimba   khuyimba   verenga   ᎤᎠᏆᎶ

er   shoma   syooma   il -wäch wuj   ✕Ꭹᕈ   łaoza   Agidôzik

ee   lére   keraneskin   balelezi   wilika   lezen   ಓದು   darllen

ांचवुं   thoma   heluhelu   chetinàv   ארק   "...is to Read."

ʔ\&@0| qillqarimay   léigh   okumak   leggiri   "Read?"

ai'tau   ilok ru hu   읽다   ᚱᚠᛈᚾᛂ   ropead

iren   lesha   pule   Skaitīt   leger   Lego

ugema   ikulosha   Legibilis   Exi   membaca   I

namaky   lenn   చదువు   Lukea   ⲞⲔⲉⲰⲘⲅⲓⲅⲁⲙⲁ   ask.

iyeem ntawv   liladön   አንብብ   igri   جنّقُو

կարդալ Оҡу karanta إِقْرَأْ lees чытаць

čitati కెఉవోఏ kenkan 读 讀 číst পড়া

oxumaq बांच lire basahin igri dubbisuu

le ၥၬၣၥၥၥၬၥ পঢ় lesen διαβάστε পঢ়ঁ

לקרא olvas lesa ᜃ ᜑᜐ پڑ léamh

خواندن leia citit читать moñe'ê preberite leer kusoma lä

อ่าน ವಾಚಿ читати پڑھیں đọc پڑھن വായിക്കുക еджэ

𒀀 ؤلوله malꓛИngw3t lexoj te pānui i ອ່ານ kuwereng

Sewawʌnahnó·tu lleer soma valaanga مدمـ(ٵٮ murun k

ᐊᕐᒡᖅ taaNga خوان ئوقيرغا bala kasyn апхьар

ᐅᖃᓕᒪᖅᑐᖅ पढ़नु морафтомс унших oserí 'nena kubal

taitai wawijge' वाचणे leysi irakurri 𒀭 𒁉 𒐊 𒐊 lukō

il -wäch wuj tidi caw 𐎀𐎁 adástl'ish k'é wusdyeh diesha les

legi tcidu پڑھنا eadray cenda cxitat پڑھنڑ leseat lj

rubead t'khiro kuvazya lhaih chijkatun ·-...-· :·:·:· ⱳⱳ

uku-wazya वच् ئوقۇمـاق egiljet igri ilhun lektar leze

"Read," says the teacher again.

"When you read
you learn
and when you learn
you grow
and when you grow
you can do things
and when you can do things
you help yourself
and when you help yourself
you can help other people,
and this is the **Secret of Life."**

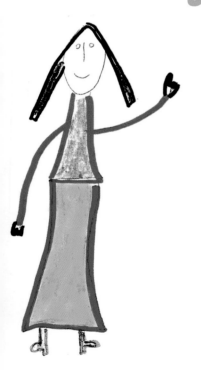

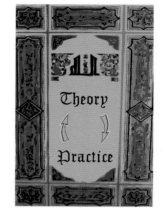

"Can I learn forever?" I hope.
"Yes Khadijah, learning is forever,
not just when you're small. Your
whole life is like a big, gigantic school.
You will learn many things everywhere,
not just in the classroom."

"Everywhere?"
"Yes Khadijah, everywhere really means
every where.

The many things you will read, see, hear,
smell, and feel are part of your learning.

Learning is a responsibility.
You must use what you have learned to be better.
It all begins with reading because

reading is the
Mother of all learning.

I love being a student

Learning is Forever

You'll always be a
student no matter
where you are.

Look at me; I'm still learning
everywhere I go because I love
being a student!

For the first time, I finally understand what **everyone** is saying.

show me
And I shall see...

I can learn too!

Fun!

Help myself...

Help other people...

YAY!!!

I won't have butterflies anymore; I'll play with the pink monkeys and I'll stop crying. The teacher is right. It all starts with reading, and then it becomes much much more!

I'm going to learn so I help myself do things, and so I can help other people do things.

I really will remember the Secret of Life!

Before the teacher can say anything, I **smile** and say,
"**Don't be silly**, you go to school because you
learn so so so much!"

Questions

The story

1. What did you learn from the story?
2. What does "Baba" mean? What language or languages do you think the word "Baba" comes from?
3. What places do you think Khadijah visited during her family vacation?
4. If you were Khadijah's parents, how would you have helped her? Likewise, if you were Khadijah's teacher, how would you have helped Khadijah?
5. Why does the book open from right to left?
6. Look at the "Read" scene, pages 18-19. Share a story based on a language experience you identify with.

School/Education

7. How do/did you feel about starting school? What are some feelings you have when you go to school? How do you cope with these feelings?
8. The poem on the back cover says no one is "uneducated" and that "Education doesn't follow standards; rather, standards follow Education." Moreover, on the title page, it states "Education means you help yourse What does education mean to you? Who defines it? How do you define it? What have you learned that ha made you better? Share a success story.
9. When you learn, do you read/learn from one or many sources? Why?
10. Human Potential is endless possibilities to be. The "Read" scene, pages 18-19 is a visual reflection of Human Potential. Observe how the concept of "Read" is reflected in over 200 ways (languages/pictures/symbols). There are roughly 6500 spoken languages in the world today. If one concept can be developed in so many ways, Human Potential becomes a critical fact. How can/does this truth relate to you?
11. The plaque on page 20 shows a continuous relationship of theory to practice and then more theory for mo practice. How do you interpret this cycle? Can you think of an example?

Life Skills/Personal Development/Reflection

12. When you go to a new place, how do you try to feel comfortable?
13. Time management is critical for progress. Share strategies you know of that work.
14. If you recognize a name that sounds different or looks different, do you say it as you read it, or do you ask that person how to say his or her name? If you have a name that is said in a special way, do you tell people how it's said?
15. Design a program that can help other people. Document and share your concept.
16. If you wrote a book, what would you write about?
17. Pink monkeys represent the unknown. What is the unknown? How do you prepare for the unknown?
18. What are words or phrases you identify with on the inside front cover? Reflect or share.
19. What would you do if you realized you were wrong about something? What advice would you give yourse
20. Consistency is a key ingredient for progress and achieving results. Yet to achieve consistency, one must be motivated. How do you get motivated? How can motivation be prolonged?
21. If there is at least one thing you want to do in your life, what is it? What are you going to do about it?

IDEAS

True Effort

never lies

True Effort

never dies

CHANGE

WORLD